Dear Parent:

W9-CHN-944

Congratulations! Your child is taking the first steps on an exciting journey. The destination? Independent reading!

STEP INTO READING® will help your child get there. The program offers books at five levels that accompany children from their first attempts at reading to reading success. Each step includes fun stories, fiction and nonfiction, and colorful art. There are also Step into Reading Sticker Books, Step into Reading Math Readers, and Step into Reading Phonics Readers— a complete literacy program with something to interest every child.

Learning to Read, Step by Step!

Ready to Read Preschool–Kindergarten
• big type and easy words • rhyme and rhythm • picture clues
For children who know the alphabet and are eager to begin reading.

Reading with Help Preschool–Grade 1
• basic vocabulary • short sentences • simple stories
For children who recognize familiar words and sound out new words with help.

Reading on Your Own Grades 1–3
• engaging characters • easy-to-follow plots • popular topics
For children who are ready to read on their own.

Reading Paragraphs Grades 2–3
• challenging vocabulary • short paragraphs • exciting stories
For newly independent readers who read simple sentences with confidence.

Ready for Chapters Grades 2–4
• chapters • longer paragraphs • full-color art
For children who want to take the plunge into chapter books but still like colorful pictures.

STEP INTO READING® is designed to give every child a successful reading experience. The grade levels are only guides. Children can progress through the steps at their own speed, developing confidence in their reading, no matter what their grade.

Remember, a lifetime love of reading starts with a single step!

To Jeff
—L.H.B.

Text copyright © 2001 by Linda Hayward. Illustrations copyright © 2001 by Laura Huliska-Beith. All rights reserved under International and Pan-American Copyright Conventions. Published in the United States by Random House Children's Books, a division of Random House, Inc., New York, and simultaneously in Canada by Random House of Canada Limited, Toronto. Originally published by Golden Books, an imprint of Random House Children's Books, a division of Random House, Inc., New York, in 2001.

www.stepintoreading.com

Educators and librarians, for a variety of teaching tools, visit us at www.randomhouse.com/teachers

Library of Congress Cataloging-in-Publication Data
Hayward, Linda. Pepe and Papa / by Linda Hayward ; illustrated by Laura Huliska-Beith.
    p.   cm. — (Step into reading. A step 1 book)
SUMMARY: In this adaptation of a familiar story, a father and son take the advice of different people on how they should carry their chiles to market.
ISBN 0-307-26114-X (trade) — ISBN 0-307-46114-9 (lib. bdg.)
[1. Folklore.]   I. Huliska-Beith, Laura, ill.   II. Title.   III. Series: Step into reading. Step 1 book.
PZ8.1.H3245 Pe 2003   398.22—dc21   2002013660

Printed in the United States of America   12 11 10 9 8 7 6 5 4 3
First Random House Edition.

STEP INTO READING, RANDOM HOUSE, and the Random House colophon are registered trademarks of Random House, Inc.

STEP INTO READING®

STEP
1

Pepe and Papa

By Linda Hayward

Illustrated by

Laura Huliska-Beith

Random House New York

Chiles on bushes.

Chiles in basket.

Basket on burro.

To market we go.

No, no!
Poor Pepe!

Chiles in basket.
Basket on Papa.

Pepe on burro.

To market we go.

No, no!
Poor Papa!

Chiles in basket.
Basket on Pepe.

Papa on burro.

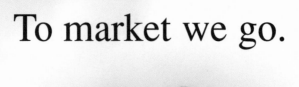

To market we go.

No, no!
Poor burro!

Chiles in basket.
Basket on burro.

Burro on Papa!

To market we—

Papa in bushes.
Pepe in basket.

Chiles in burro.
Oh, oh!